CW00687730

# PUBLISH WITH PURPOSE

# Publish with Purpose

## A ROADMAP TO BESTSELLING SUCCESS

B. Vincent

QuillQuest Publishers

# *Contents*

# 1

# Chapter 1: The Evolution of Publishing

The Beginning of Distributing

Before all else, the scattering of information and stories was an oral custom, dependent on memory and vocal transmission starting with one age then onto the next. This strategy, while private, was loaded with restrictions, prominently the gamble of adjustment over the long haul and topographical imperatives. The creation of composing frameworks denoted the primary transformation in distributing, empowering the recording of contemplations, stories, and information on materials like papyrus, mud tablets, and later, material.

The Print machine Insurgency

The following huge jump accompanied Johannes Gutenberg's creation of the versatile sort print machine in the fifteenth hundred years. This development democratized information, making books more available and reasonable. It prepared for the Edification and the Logical Transformation, time frames set apart by a phenomenal blast of information and thoughts.

The Modern Age and Large scale manufacturing

The Modern Insurgency achieved innovative progressions that further changed distributing. Steam-controlled presses and later, the advancement of typesetting machines, took into account quicker and less expensive creation of books. This time saw the ascent of periodicals, papers, and the novel as a famous scholarly structure, extending proficiency and perusing for joy to more extensive crowds.

The twentieth 100 years: Enhancement and Specialization

The twentieth century presented new types of media, like radio, TV, and later, the web, which rivaled books for individuals' consideration. In spite of this, the distributing business kept on developing, expanding into different types and specialties. Distributers turned out to be more particular, zeroing in on unambiguous classifications or kinds of books, from instructive materials to sci-fi and dream.

The Advanced Upset

The coming of the web and computerized innovation denoted another time for distributing. The send off of Amazon in 1994 and the presentation of the main tablet gadgets in the mid 2000s changed how books were circulated and consumed. Advanced distributing considered the moment dispersion of digital books, fundamentally bringing down creation and circulation expenses and making distributing more available to writers through independently publishing stages.

The Ascent of Independently publishing

Advanced stages have enabled writers to sidestep conventional distributing courses, offering apparatuses for distributing, dissemination, and showcasing straightforwardly to perusers. Independently publishing has turned into a practical way to progress, as confirmed by creators like Amanda Selling and Hugh Howey, who have accomplished critical deals and praise. This shift has constrained customary distributers to adjust, prompting changes in agreements, eminence rates, and advertising techniques.

The Effect on Creators

The development of distributing significantly affects creators, offering more pathways to distribution and difficulties in sticking out. Conventional distributing offers the advantages of expert altering, plan, and promoting support, yet with additional critical boundaries to passage and frequently more slow courses to advertise. Interestingly, independently publishing offers more prominent control and possibly higher eminences, however expects creators to assume the jobs of distributer and advertiser.

Latest things and Future Headings

The distributing business keeps on developing, with patterns like book recordings and webcasts acquiring prominence. Membership models and direct deals through writer sites are turning out to be more normal, offering writers higher eminences and direct commitment with perusers. The fate of distributing may see further mixing of media, with books venturing into intelligent and sight and sound encounters.

# 2

# Chapter 2: Traditional vs. Self-Publishing

The distributing scene remains at a junction, characterized by two essential ways a creator can take: conventional distributing and independently publishing. Every way offers special advantages and difficulties, and understanding these can assist creators with arriving at informed conclusions about which course best lines up with their objectives, assets, and inclinations.

Grasping Conventional Distributing

Customary distributing alludes to the traditional course of collaborating with laid out distributing houses to put up a book for sale to the public. This way is frequently viewed as lofty and offers different benefits yet in addition accompanies its arrangement of constraints.

The Professionals of Customary Distributing

1. Professional Altering and Plan: Distributers give proficient altering, cover plan, and designing administrations, guaranteeing the book satisfies industry guidelines.
2. Marketing and Dissemination: Laid out distributers have broad conveyance organizations, putting books in significant retailers and book shops. They additionally offer promoting support, albeit the degree can shift contingent upon the writer's profile and the book's apparent business potential.
3. Advances and Eminences: Creators normally get a development against sovereignties, giving forthright installment. Sovereignties on book deals follow, however these rates are much of the time lower than independently publishing.
4. Credibility and Esteem: Being distributed by a perceived distributing house can improve a creator's standing, opening up potential open doors for talking commitment, meetings, and that's just the beginning.

The Cons of Conventional Distributing

1. Competitive and Tedious: Getting a distributing bargain is profoundly cutthroat, frequently requiring a specialist. The cycle from accommodation to distribution can require years.
2. Less Imaginative Control: Creators have restricted say in perspectives like cover configuration, showcasing methodology, and here and there happy, which can prompt conflicts.
3. Financial Returns: The monetary advantages can be unassuming for new creators, with propels being low and sovereignties a little level of deals.

Exploring Independently publishing

Independently publishing has arisen as a strong other option, offering control and possibly higher monetary returns. This way permits creators to distribute their work straightforwardly to stages like Amazon's Encourage Direct Distributing, bypassing customary guardians.

The Experts of Independently publishing

1. Creative Control: Writers hold full oversight over their book's substance, plan, and promoting procedure, taking into consideration a more customized approach.
2. Higher Sovereignties: Independently published writers can procure fundamentally higher eminences per book, frequently 50-70% of the deal value, contrasted with the customary course.
3. Speed to Market: Without the requirement for specialists or distributers, writers can put up their books for sale to the public rapidly, some of the time very quickly.
4. Flexibility: Independently publishing offers the adaptability to explore different avenues regarding various classes, cover plans, and evaluating systems to find what works best.

The Cons of Independently publishing

1. Upfront Expenses: Creators are answerable for the expenses of altering, cover configuration, designing, and showcasing, which can add up.
2. Marketing and Dissemination: While computerized stages offer impressive range, actual conveyance is restricted. Advertising falls completely on the creator, requiring critical exertion and skill.
3. Quality Worries: Without proficient altering and plan, independently published books can experience in quality, affecting deals and notoriety.

4. Discoverability: Hanging out in a packed market is a test, with many books never getting forward momentum.

Picking the Best Way

The choice among conventional and independently publishing relies upon a few variables, including the creator's objectives, assets, and obligation to promoting. For those looking for glory and will explore the cutthroat scene, conventional distributing might be the way. On the other hand, independently publishing is appropriate for creators wanting control and higher sovereignties, if they are ready to put resources into quality and showcasing.

Key Contemplations

•Objectives and Assumptions: Characterize what achievement resembles, whether it's contacting a wide crowd, accomplishing monetary freedom, or earning respect in a particular field.

•Assets and Abilities: Evaluate the assets accessible for interest in the independently publishing process and the abilities to showcase the book actually.

•Market Getting it: Exploration the market interest for the book's type or point, understanding where it might have a superior potential for success of progress.

The decision among conventional and independently publishing is definitely not a one-size-fits-all choice. It requires a cautious assessment of individual objectives, assets, and the compromises every way offers. By understanding these perspectives, writers can settle on informed choices, preparing for their book's prosperity, no matter what the picked distributing course.

# 3

# Chapter 3: Crafting Your Manuscript

Creating a composition is the foundation of your excursion to distribution. This part digs into the complexities of composing, altering, and setting up your original copy for distribution. By underlining quality substance, we mean to direct writers through the careful course of changing thoughts into a cleaned, prepared to-distribute composition.

Beginning with a Strong Groundwork

Before you type the primary word, having an unmistakable vision and an organized arrangement for your composition is significant. This establishment will direct your creative cycle, assist with keeping up with center, and guarantee soundness in your narrating or piece.

1. Characterize Your Motivation and Crowd

•Comprehend the center message of your book and the crowd you plan to reach. This clearness will shape your composing style, tone, and content.

2. Frame Your Composition

•Make a nitty gritty diagram, isolating your book into segments, sections, and central issues. This guide will keep you coordinated and make the creative cycle more reasonable.

Composing Your Composition

With a strong groundwork set up, you can set out on the composing venture. This stage is tied in with transforming your diagram into an undeniable original copy, a cycle that requires discipline, imagination, and adaptability.

1. Lay out a Composing Schedule

•Put forth reasonable composing objectives and a timetable that accommodates your way of life. Consistency is critical to gaining consistent headway.

2. Embrace the Principal Draft

•Permit yourself to compose openly in the principal draft, zeroing in on getting your thoughts down without agonizing over flawlessness.

3. Look for Input Early

•Share your work with confided in beta perusers or composing gatherings to acquire significant experiences and points of view. This criticism can be instrumental in distinguishing qualities and regions for development.

Altering and Cleaning

Altering is where your composition goes through change, developing from a work in progress to a cleaned piece prepared for distribution. This stage is much of the time testing however is basic in upgrading the quality and comprehensibility of your book.

1. Self-Altering Strategies

•Begin with significant level alters zeroing in on construction, pacing, and consistency. Then, move to line alters for language structure, punctuation, and style.

2. Proficient Altering

•Consider putting resources into proficient altering administrations. An expert manager can offer important experiences and rectifications that may be ignored by the creator.

3. Integrate Input Admirably

•Return to the input from your beta perusers and supervisor. Conclude which ideas line up with your vision for the book and make changes likewise.

Getting ready for Distribution

When your composition is altered and cleaned, now is the ideal time to set it up supposed to be available for the public. This last step includes a few critical undertakings to guarantee your book satisfies industry guidelines and is prepared for perusers.

1. Arranging Your Original copy

•Design your composition as indicated by the necessities of your picked distributing stage. This might differ between digital books and print books.

2. Picking the Right Title and Cover

•Your book's title and cover are the principal things potential perusers will see. Pick a title that mirrors the substance of your book and a cover plan that draws in your interest group.

3. Composing a Convincing Book Depiction

•Make a book portrayal that gives an unmistakable and tempting outline of your book's substance. This is essential for spellbinding possible perusers.

4. Acquiring ISBNs and Copyrights

•Secure an ISBN for your book, which is fundamental for dissemination and deals following. Also, consider enlisting your copyright to safeguard your work.

Creating your composition is an excursion of change, from the underlying idea to a cleaned book prepared for distribution. By keeping these rules on composition, altering, and setting up your original copy, you position your work for outcome in the serious universe of distributing. Quality substance is fundamental, and with devotion, your composition can tolerate outing and spellbind the hearts and psyches of perusers.

# 4

# Chapter 4: Building Your Author Platform

In the present computerized age, having serious areas of strength for a stage is fundamental for interfacing with your crowd, advancing your work, and building a supportable composing vocation. This section investigates extensive procedures for laying out and upgrading your web-based presence, utilizing online entertainment, making an individual site, and compelling systems administration to draw in with your perusers and industry experts.

Grasping the Creator Stage

A creator stage is a blend of instruments and channels that permits creators to feature their work, draw in with their crowd, and construct their image. A vigorous stage expands your perceivability, believability, and impact in the scholarly local area.

1. The Significance of a Creator Stage

•It fills in as the establishment for showcasing and advancing your books.

•Upgrades discoverability to possible perusers and industry partners.

•Works with direct correspondence and commitment with your crowd.

Building Serious areas of strength for a Presence

A solid web-based presence is vital to a fruitful creator stage. It includes making content and drawing in with your crowd across different advanced mediums.

1. Virtual Entertainment Authority

•Pick the Right Stages: Spotlight via virtual entertainment stages where your main interest group is generally dynamic. For most writers, this incorporates stages like Twitter, Instagram, Facebook, and conceivably TikTok or LinkedIn.

•Connect Really: Consistently post content that draws in your crowd — blend limited time material in with individual experiences, composing tips, and in the background looks at your career as a writer.

•Assemble Connections: Utilize online entertainment to associate with individual creators, distributers, and powerhouses in your kind. Commitment and cooperation can essentially extend your scope.

2. Fostering an Individual Site

•Make an Expert Site: Your site ought to incorporate a memoir, a list of your work, a blog, and contact data. It fills in as the center of your web-based presence.

•Quality written substance is the final deciding factor: Update your site routinely with blog entries, news, and updates about your composition. Search engine oriented content can likewise assist with expanding your site's perceivability on web indexes.

•Pamphlet Recruits: Urge guests to pursue your bulletin. Email showcasing is an immediate line to your perusers, considering customized correspondence and advancement.

3. Writing for a blog and Visitor Posting

•Lay out Power: Standard publishing content to a blog on your site or visitor posting on different locales can lay out you as an expert in your classification or industry.

•Drive Commitment: Offer your web journals via online entertainment and draw in with perusers who remark. This connection cultivates local area and makes perusers want more.

Systems administration and Local area Commitment

Past the computerized domain, individual connections and systems administration assume an essential part in building your creator stage.

1. Go to Artistic Occasions and Meetings

•Cooperation in abstract occasions, book fairs, and composing gatherings can give important openness and systems administration valuable open doors.

•Speaking Commitment: Proposing to talk at occasions or partake in boards can upgrade your profile and draw in a following.

2. Join Composing Gatherings and Affiliations

•Being important for composing gatherings and expert affiliations can offer help, assets, and systems administration open doors.

•Joint effort and Cross-Advancement: Team up with different creators for cross-advancement, profiting from shared crowds.

Utilizing Audits and Supports

Positive audits and supports from regarded figures in the scholarly local area can essentially reinforce your creator stage.

1. Request Audits: Urge perusers to leave surveys on stages like Amazon and Goodreads. Authentic peruser surveys can support your book's perceivability and validity.

2. Look for Supports: Supports from notable creators or industry experts can loan huge load to your work. These can be included on your book cover, site, and limited time materials.

Observing and Adjusting Your System

Building a creator stage is a continuous interaction that requires observing and transformation to changing patterns and crowd inclinations.

1. Break down Commitment: Use investigation devices to follow commitment on your site and web-based entertainment. Understanding what content reverberates with your crowd can direct your technique.

2. Remain Current: Stay up to date with recent fads and stages in advanced advertising. Adjusting to the advanced scene can keep your foundation dynamic and locking in.

A solid creator stage is fundamental for present day creators intending to contact a more extensive crowd and lay out an effective profession. By decisively constructing your web-based presence, drawing in with your local area, and utilizing organizing valuable open doors, you can make a strong stage that upholds your composing tries and encourages enduring associations with your perusers.

# 5

# Chapter 5: Understanding Your Audience

In the domain of distributing, a profound comprehension of your main interest group is vital. This information shapes the making of your work as well as illuminates your showcasing procedures, guaranteeing they reverberate with the perusers probably going to draw in with your book. This part investigates compelling methods for distinguishing and grasping your objective readership, empowering you to tailor your methodologies for most extreme effect.

The Significance of Crowd Understanding

Perceiving your crowd goes past segment information; it's tied in with grasping their inclinations, inclinations, difficulties, and what they look for in a book. This understanding impacts the substance of your composition as well as the manner in which you present and advance your work.

1. Crowd Knowledge Powers Importance

•Fitting substance and advertising messages to match crowd interests guarantees importance, essentially improving commitment and reaction rates.

2. Guides Showcasing and Circulation Endeavors

•Understanding what where your listeners might be thinking invests their energy, both on the web and disconnected, helps in picking the right channels for showcasing and dispersion.

Recognizing Your Interest group

The most important phase in understanding your crowd is distinguishing what their identity is. This interaction includes a blend of examination, investigation, and at times, instinct.

1. Examine Existing Perusers

•Assuming that you have distributed previously, examine your current peruser base through audits, virtual entertainment commitment, and direct input.

2. Lead Statistical surveying

•Use statistical surveying apparatuses and stages like Google Patterns, Amazon's Smash hits records, and virtual entertainment examination to assemble information on expected perusers.

3. Make Peruser Personas

•Foster itemized personas addressing your optimal perusers. Incorporate socioeconomics, interests, understanding propensities, and whatever other important data that customizes your promoting messages.

Figuring out Crowd Inclinations

When you have an unmistakable image of your interest group, dive further into figuring out their inclinations and ways of behaving.

1. Connect Straightforwardly with Perusers

•Use virtual entertainment, email pamphlets, and peruser reviews to pose direct inquiries about their inclinations and criticism on your work.

2. Screen Patterns and Conversations

•Remain dynamic in web-based gatherings, book clubs, and online entertainment bunches where your ideal interest group assembles. Noticing conversations and patterns can offer bits of knowledge into their ongoing advantages.

3. Investigate Contenders

•Take a gander at books and writers in your classification that are effective with your interest group. Dissect their subjects, promoting strategies, and peruser commitment to distinguish what requests to your crowd.

Fitting Promoting Techniques

With an exhaustive comprehension of your crowd, you can now tailor your showcasing procedures to talk straightforwardly to their inclinations and necessities.

1. Redo Your Informing

•Create promoting messages that address the particular interests, difficulties, or wants of your crowd, making your book the arrangement they look for.

2. Pick the Right Showcasing Channels

•Select advertising channels where your crowd is generally dynamic. This could be web-based entertainment stages, email promoting, sites, digital broadcasts, or customary media, contingent upon your crowd's inclinations.

3. Offer Worth Past the Book

•Consider what extra worth you can offer your perusers, like related articles, studios, or online occasions, to draw in them further and construct a local area around your work.

Checking and Adjusting

Understanding your crowd is certainly not a one-time task however a continuous interaction. As patterns shift and new data arises, it's fundamental for screen crowd commitment and adjust your techniques as needs be.

1. Track Commitment and Criticism

•Routinely audit the presentation of your showcasing endeavors and the input from your crowd to measure what's working and what isn't.

2. Remain Open to Advancement

•Be ready to advance comprehension you might interpret your crowd and your promoting techniques as recent fads arise and as you accumulate more information on what resounds with your perusers.

Getting a handle on the subtleties of your main interest group is a basic part of distributing achievement. By utilizing the methods framed in this part to distinguish, comprehend, and draw in your crowd, you can make promoting systems that successfully resound with your perusers. This grasping not just guides in the effective advancement of your ongoing work yet additionally lays the foundation for building a reliable peruser base for future distributions.

# 6

# Chapter 6: Navigating the Publishing Process

Exploring the distributing system, whether through customary or independently publishing courses, can be a complex and nuanced venture. This part intends to demystify the means in question, offering an unmistakable, bit by bit guide from composition accommodation to the second your book contacts its crowd. By seeing each stage, creators can pursue informed choices and explore the interaction with certainty.

Customary Distributing Cycle

The customary distributing course includes presenting your composition to distributers or artistic specialists, who will then, at that point, assume on the liability of altering, delivering, conveying, and advertising your book. This way offers the advantage of industry mastery yet requires persistence and a readiness to give up some command over the distributing system.

1. Setting up Your Accommodation

•Research specialists or distributers that line up with your type and crowd.

•Set up a convincing question letter, an outline of your book, and a cleaned original copy test as indicated by their accommodation rules.

2. Accommodation Interaction

•Present your materials to chose specialists or distributers.

•Hope to hang tight for reactions, which can require a while.

3. Getting a Distributing Arrangement

•On the off chance that a specialist or distributer shows interest, you might get a proposition. This regularly includes dealings on advances, sovereignties, and privileges.

•Marking an agreement formalizes the arrangement, framing the details of your organization.

4. Altering and Creation

•Work with the distributer's article group to refine your original copy.

•The distributer will deal with the plan, arranging, and creation of your book.

5. Showcasing and Conveyance

•Distributers will foster a showcasing plan, which might incorporate book visits, special materials, and official statements.

•Your book will be circulated through the distributer's channels, arriving at book shops and online retailers.

Independently publishing Interaction

Independently publishing gives creators unlimited authority over the distributing system, from altering and plan to promoting and deals. While it offers more noteworthy artistic liberty and possibly higher sovereignties, it additionally requires critical exertion and speculation.

1. Finishing Your Original copy

•Guarantee your composition is completely altered, either by self-altering or recruiting an expert manager.

2. Plan and Designing

•Plan an expert cover that catches the substance of your book and requests to your interest group.

•Design your composition for digital book as well as print, complying to stage explicit rules.

3. Picking a Distributing Stage

•Research and select an independently publishing stage that suits your objectives, for example, Amazon's Encourage Direct Distributing, IngramSpark, or Smashwords.

4. Distribution

•Transfer your original copy and cover plan to the picked stage, set your cost, and distribute. Your book will be ready to move as indicated by the stage's course of events, frequently in practically no time.

5. Showcasing and Appropriation

•Create and execute a showcasing plan, using web-based entertainment, email advertising, book surveys, and different techniques to advance your book.

•Consider extra appropriation channels, like individual sites or neighborhood book shops, to grow your compass.

Crossover Distributing and Different Contemplations

Notwithstanding customary and independently publishing, half breed models offer a mix of both, giving proficient distributing administrations to a charge. This choice can be a center ground for creators looking for proficient help without going through the customary accommodation process.

Lawful and Monetary Contemplations

No matter what the distributing course, it's critical to figure out the lawful and monetary angles, including copyright, agreements, expenses, and sovereignty the executives. Instructing yourself on these points or looking for proficient guidance can safeguard your inclinations and guarantee a smooth distributing venture.

The way from original copy to distributed book is laden with choices, from picking the right distributing course to dealing with the complexities of creation and promoting. By understanding the means associated with both conventional and independently publishing processes, creators can explore these waters no sweat and certainty, guaranteeing their work contacts the crowd it merits.

# 7

# Chapter 7: Design and Formatting for Success

In the excursion of distributing a book, the meaning of expert plan and organizing couldn't possibly be more significant. These components not just improve the comprehensibility and tasteful allure of your book yet additionally assume a vital part in drawing in and holding perusers' advantage. This part dives into the significance of cover plan, inside design, and computerized organizing, giving writers fundamental experiences for guaranteeing their book hangs out in a packed commercial center.

The Force of Cover Plan

The proverb "don't pass judgment without giving it at least some forethought" doesn't turn out as expected in the distributing scene. A cover is much of the time the primary connection a potential peruser has with your book, making it a basic showcasing device.

1. Visual Allure

•An expertly planned cover catches consideration and creates interest. It ought to mirror the book's classification and tone, interesting to the ideal interest group.

2. Brand Consistency

•For writers with various works, reliable plan components across books can assist with laying out memorability.

3. Incredible skill

•A great cover signs to perusers that a similar degree of care has been applied to the substance inside.

Dominating Inside Design

The inside format of your book assumes an imperative part in giving a consistent understanding encounter. Proficient organizing guarantees that the text is open, connecting with, and liberated from interruptions.

1. Meaningfulness

•Appropriate utilization of text styles, dividing, and edges makes the text simple to peruse. Decisions ought to be made with the interest group's inclinations and necessities as a main priority.

2. Stylish Agreement

•The inside plan ought to supplement the cover and the book's subject, making a strong tasteful from one cover to another.

3. Navigational Clearness

•Components like the list of chapters, headers, footers, and section titles ought to be plainly organized to direct perusers through the book.

Exploring Computerized Organizing Prerequisites

With the ascent of digital books, understanding computerized organizing has become fundamental. Advanced designs require explicit contemplations to guarantee similarity across different tablets and gadgets.

1. Responsive Plan

•digital books ought to be designed to permit text and pictures to change flawlessly to various screen sizes and directions.

2. Intelligent Components

•Contingent upon the stage, writers can improve digital books with hyperlinks, sound, video, and intuitive elements, advancing the understanding experience.

3. Stage Explicit Rules

•Look into the organizing rules of each advanced distributing stage. Consistence guarantees that your book works accurately on every gadget and dissemination channel.

Employing Experts versus Do-It-Yourself

While certain writers might be enticed to handle plan and arranging themselves, recruiting experts can essentially affect the book's attractiveness and achievement.

1. Proficient Ability

•Architects and formatters acquire aptitude industry guidelines, patterns, and specialized necessities, guaranteeing your book fulfills proficient quality guidelines.

2. Time and Cost Effectiveness

•Experts can finish the work all the more effectively, permitting writers to zero in on composition and promoting. While there is a forthright expense, the speculation can take care of in the book's show and deals.

3. Customization and Innovativeness

•Working with experts gives amazing open doors to customization and innovativeness that may not be feasible through Do-It-Yourself techniques or format based plan instruments.

Best Practices for Teaming up with Planners

Compelling joint effort with creators and formatters is critical to accomplishing your vision for the book.

1. Clear Correspondence

•Give a reasonable brief and be explicit about your assumptions, including subjects, colors, and a particular plan components you imagine.

2. Be Available to Ideas

•Plan experts offer significant experience that would be useful. Be available to their ideas and criticism to accomplish the best outcomes.

3. Audit and Reexamine

•Take part in a survey cycle, giving valuable criticism and permitting to modifications to refine the plan and designing until it meets your fulfillment.

The significance of expert plan and organizing in the outcome of a book can't be put into words. These components not just upgrade the book's tasteful allure and meaningfulness yet additionally contribute essentially to its attractiveness. By focusing on proficient cover plan, careful inside design, and consistent computerized organizing, writers can guarantee their book sticks out and gives an essential understanding encounter.

# 8

# Chapter 8: Marketing Your Book

Compelling showcasing is fundamental for the outcome of any book, filling in as the scaffold that associates your work with its target group. This part gives an exhaustive manual for creating and executing promoting techniques both when your book's distribution. By embracing a proactive way to deal with promoting, writers can essentially improve their book's perceivability, draw in with perusers, and lift deals.

Pre-Distribution Promoting

The promoting endeavors that go before your book's send off can fabricate expectation, make buzz, and lay out a peruser base even before your book stirs things up around town.

1. Fabricate Your Creator Stage

•Reinforce your web-based presence through virtual entertainment, your own site, and publishing content to a blog. Draw in with your crowd by sharing experiences into your creative cycle, book mysteries, and individual stories.

2. Cover Uncover and Pre-orders

•Produce fervor by uncovering your book cover early. Set up pre-orders on your site and online retailers, offering impetuses like marked duplicates or selective substance to early purchasers.

3. Content Promoting

•Use content promoting by distributing articles, blog entries, or visitor presents related on your book's topic or topic. This technique can draw in perusers keen on your book's class or point.

4. Email Promoting

•Foster an email showcasing effort to keep your crowd educated and locked in. Share refreshes, select reviews, and unique proposals with your supporters.

5. Network with Powerhouses and Bloggers

•Lay out associations with powerhouses and bloggers who take care of your interest group. Their supports can altogether widen your compass.

Send off Techniques

Your book's send off is a basic period that requires centered showcasing endeavors to boost effect and deals.

1. Send off Occasion

•Sort out a send off occasion, either face to face or virtual, to praise the delivery. This can incorporate readings, back and forth discussions, and collaborations with your crowd.

2. Online Entertainment Rush

•Coordinate a virtual entertainment rush on your send off day. Use every one of your foundation to make a buzz, empowering offers, and commitment from your devotees.

3. Public statement

•Disseminate an official statement declaring your book's delivery to news sources, book web journals, and industry distributions.

4. Limited time Offers

•Offer time-restricted special arrangements, like limited evaluating or packaged offers, to help introductory deals.

Post-Send off Promoting

The promoting exertion shouldn't stop post-send off. Consistent advancement is critical to supporting deals energy and building a drawn out peruser base.

1. Book Audits

•Urge perusers to leave audits on Amazon, Goodreads, and different stages. Positive surveys can altogether impact likely purchasers.

2. Creator Appearances

•Partake in book signings, artistic celebrations, and talking occasions to keep your book in the public eye.

3. Use Paid Publicizing

•Think about utilizing paid publicizing choices via online entertainment stages, Amazon, or Google to contact a more extensive crowd.

4. Influence Book Grants and Contests

•Present your book to grants and contests. Wins or selections can support your book's validity and perceivability.

Long haul Showcasing Procedures

Supporting revenue in your book over the long haul requires continuous exertion and imaginative advertising methodologies.

1. Content Updates and Side projects

•Keep your crowd connected by delivering related content, for example, veer off stories, character profound plunges, or in the background takes a gander at your creative cycle.

2. Cross-Advancement

•Collaborate with different creators for cross-advancement open doors. This can incorporate group bargains, joint occasions, or online entertainment takeovers.

3. Reuse Content

•Reuse your book's substance into various arrangements, for example, blog entries, digital recordings, or recordings to arrive at various sections of your crowd.

Showcasing your book is a dynamic and progressing process that ranges from the pre-distribution stage through the book send off and well into the post-send off time frame. By utilizing a blend of vital promoting endeavors, writers can really expand their book's perceivability, interface with perusers, and drive deals. Fitting your way to deal with fit your book's kind, crowd, and your own image will yield the best outcomes, transforming your distributing venture into an effective undertaking.

# 9

# Chapter 9: The Role of Book Reviews

Book surveys assume a vital part in the outcome of a distribution, affecting perusers' buying choices and essentially affecting deals. Positive surveys can improve a book's perceivability and believability, while an expansive range of audits can give important criticism to writers. This part investigates techniques to collect book surveys, exploring the intricacies of audit stages, and utilizing audits to support book deals.

Figuring out the Effect of Audits

Audits go about as friendly confirmation, offering potential perusers bits of knowledge into others' encounters with your book. They can feature your book's assets, assisting uncertain perusers with pursuing the buy choice.

1. Perceivability through Calculations

•Numerous web-based retailers, including Amazon, use calculations that figure the number and nature of surveys to decide a book's perceivability in list items and proposals.

2. Validity and Trust

•Audits from perusers and legitimate pundits can loan validity to your book, building entrust with expected perusers.

Methodologies for Gathering Audits

Acquiring surveys requires exertion and system, particularly for new creators or those distributing freely.

1. Advance Survey Duplicates (Bends)

•Appropriate Bends to book bloggers, analysts, and perusers before your book's true delivery. This can prompt surveys being accessible at send off, giving a quick lift.

2. Influence Web-based Entertainment and Online People group

•Use your web-based entertainment stages and online networks to demand surveys from your adherents who are keen on your kind.

3. Draw in with Book Survey Bloggers and Powerhouses

•Exploration and contact book bloggers and powerhouses with a critical continuing in your book's classification. Offer them a free duplicate in return for a legitimate survey.

4. Use Book Survey Sites and Administrations

•Sites like Goodreads, NetGalley, and BookSirens offer stages where writers can list their books for audit. A few administrations might require a charge yet can be viable in arriving at energetic perusers.

5. Consolidate Solicitations for Audits in Your Book

•Cordially request that perusers think about leaving a survey toward the finish of your book. A basic, direct solicitation can urge fulfilled perusers to share their considerations.

Exploring Survey Stages

Various stages have various approaches and crowds, making it essential to grasp the accepted procedures for each.

1. Amazon Surveys

•Amazon's survey framework is compelling however accompanies severe rules to forestall one-sided or false audits. Find out about these principles to guarantee consistency.

2. Goodreads

•Goodreads is a well known stage for perusers to find and survey books. Drawing in with the local area by making a creator profile and taking part in conversations can energize audits.

Answering Audits

Interfacing with audits, both positive and negative, can exhibit your commitment and appreciation for input.

1. Expressing gratitude toward for Positive Audits

•A straightforward thank you for positive surveys can cultivate generosity and support further commitment from perusers.

2. Dealing with Negative Surveys

•Move toward negative surveys expertly and valuably. Use them as criticism for development, however stay away from public questions which can hurt your standing.

Utilizing Audits for Showcasing

Surveys can be an integral asset in your showcasing munititions stockpile, improving special endeavors and giving substance to virtual entertainment and promoting.

1. Feature Positive Surveys

•Highlight positive audits in your advertising materials, on your site, and in virtual entertainment presents on stand out and assemble validity.

2. Use Audits in Publicizing

•Consolidating bits from gleaming surveys in your promotions can make them seriously convincing and powerful to likely perusers.

Book surveys are a crucial part of a book's prosperity, offering validity, perceivability, and important input. By effectively chasing after surveys through essential effort, drawing in with audit stages, and utilizing surveys in showcasing endeavors, writers can altogether improve their book's allure and deals potential. Taking on a proactive way to deal with surveys, while keeping up with incredible skill and appreciation, can cultivate a positive relationship with your crowd and the more extensive understanding local area.

# 10

# Chapter 10: Leveraging Social Media and Online Platforms

In the computerized age, web-based entertainment and online stages have become essential devices for writers looking to advance their books and draw in with their crowd. These stages offer extraordinary open doors for perceivability, connection, and local area building. This section frames systems for actually utilizing these computerized roads to upgrade your book's span and encourage significant associations with perusers.

Laying out Serious areas of strength for a Presence

The groundwork of compelling web-based advancement is major areas of strength for a, presence across different stages. This presence assists writers with associating with their crowd, share content, and advance their books.

1. Picking the Right Stages

•Distinguish which stages your interest group utilizes most and center your endeavors there. Well known choices incorporate Instagram for visual narrating, Twitter for speedy updates and commitment, Facebook for local area building, and LinkedIn for proficient systems administration.

2. Making Drawing in Happy

•Share content that adds worth and interests your crowd. This can incorporate in the background looks into your creative cycle, experiences into your book's subjects, character presentations, and intuitive substance like surveys or round table discussions.

3. Consistency is Vital

•Normal posting saves your crowd drew in and helps construct expectation for your book's delivery. Foster a substance schedule to design your posts and keep a reliable posting plan.

Using Web journals and Sites

An individual blog or site fills in as the center for your web-based presence, giving a space where you can share more top to bottom substance, accumulate endorsers, and concentrate your web-based exercises.

1. Content Promoting

•Utilize your blog to distribute articles connected with your book's type, subjects, or creative cycle. This content can draw in perusers keen on those points and convert them into book purchasers.

2. Website design enhancement Advancement

•Enhance your site and blog content for web indexes to increment perceivability. Utilize significant catchphrases, meta portrayals, and drawing in titles to further develop your pursuit rankings.

3. Email Records

•Urge guests to buy into your email list. Utilize this immediate line of correspondence to send refreshes, restrictive substance, and advancements to your perusers.

Drawing in with Video and Live Web based

Video content and live web based offer powerful methods for interfacing with your crowd, giving a more private and drawing in experience.

1. YouTube

•Make a YouTube channel to share recordings connected with your book, for example, readings, writer meetings, and conversations on subjects connected with your book's substance.

2. Live Streaming

•Stages like Instagram Live and Facebook Live permit you to cooperate with your crowd progressively. Have back and forth discussions, live readings, or book send off occasions to straightforwardly draw in with your perusers.

Online Entertainment Promoting

Paid online entertainment promoting can be a financially savvy method for expanding your book's perceivability and contact a bigger crowd.

1. Designated Promotions

•Stages like Facebook and Instagram offer designated publicizing choices, permitting you to arrive at explicit socioeconomics, interests, and ways of behaving, guaranteeing your advertisements are demonstrated to those probably going to be keen on your book.

2. Investigation and Improvement

•Utilize the investigation apparatuses given by online entertainment stages to follow the exhibition of your advertisements. Dissect the information to improve your promoting system for improved results.

Coordinated efforts and Organizations

Teaming up with different writers, powerhouses, and online networks can grow your scope and acquaint your book with new crowds.

1. Creator Coordinated efforts

•Band together with different creators for cross-advancement, joint live streams, or virtual occasions. This can acquaint each creator's crowd with the other's work.

2. Powerhouse Organizations

•Work with powerhouses in your kind to advance your book. Powerhouses with connected crowds can fundamentally support your book's perceivability.

Utilizing virtual entertainment and online stages is urgent for current writers intending to advance their books and interface with perusers. By laying out areas of strength for a presence, making drawing in happy, using video, putting resources into designated publicizing, and fashioning joint efforts, writers can successfully enhance their book's range and fabricate a devoted readership. In the developing scene of advanced showcasing, remaining versatile and proactive in these techniques can prompt supported achievement and perceivability for your work.

# 11

# Chapter 11: Beyond the Launch: Sustaining Book Sales

Accomplishing an effective book send off is a huge achievement, however the genuine test for the vast majority writers lies in supporting book deals past the underlying flood. The post-send off stage is basic for keeping up with energy, drawing in with perusers, and guaranteeing the drawn out progress of your book. This section frames systems to keep your book at the center of attention and support deals over the long run.

Ceaseless Commitment with Your Crowd

Drawing in with your perusers ceaselessly can assist with keeping the interest in your book alive and empower verbal exchange advancement.

1. Influence Online Entertainment

•Keep on utilizing web-based entertainment stages to share refreshes about your book, experiences into your creative cycle, and connecting with content connected with your book's subjects or characters.

2. Email Advertising

•Use your email rundown to keep your endorsers informed about your work, share select substance, and declare advancements or occasions connected with your book.

3. Intelligent Exercises

•Arrange online difficulties, giveaways, or back and forth discussions to keep your crowd drew in and intrigued by your book.

Executing Limited time Missions

Standard special missions can reignite interest in your book and draw in new perusers.

1. Limits and Restricted Time Offers

•Run time-restricted limits on your book to support buys. Feature these advancements on your web-based entertainment channels and to your email list.

2. Pack Arrangements

•Offer your book as a feature of a pack manage your different works or as a team with different writers. Packs can offer extraordinary benefit to perusers and increment deals.

3. Partake in Book Fairs and Celebrations

•Physical and virtual book fairs and celebrations can give extra perceivability and deals amazing open doors for your book.

Augmenting the Utilization of Audits and Tributes

Positive surveys and tributes are useful assets for supporting interest and confidence in your book.

1. Feature Surveys

•Consistently share positive surveys and tributes on your site, web-based entertainment, and in showcasing materials to build up the nature of your book.

2. Support Constant Surveys

•Persistently urge new perusers to leave surveys, giving new tributes that can draw in expected perusers.

Investigating Extra Income Streams

Differentiating your income streams can assist with supporting your pay from your book over the long run.

1. Book recordings and digital books

•While possibly not currently accessible, consider delivering your book in extra configurations, for example, book recording or digital book. Various arrangements can draw in various crowds.

2. Promoting

•Investigate making stock connected with your book, like banners, bookmarks, or attire. Product can upgrade your image and turn out an extra revenue stream.

3. Speaking Commitment

•Offer your administrations for talking commitment, studios, or board conversations connected with your book's point or subjects.

Keeping the Substance New

New satisfied connected with your book can assist with keeping up with interest and draw in new perusers.

1. Side projects and Spin-offs

•Consider composing side projects, spin-offs, or related books that develop your book's universe or subjects. New distributions can restore interest in your prior works.

2. Reward Content

•Discharge reward content connected with your book, like erased scenes, character histories, or an in the background take a gander at your creative cycle.

Investigating Execution and Adjusting Techniques

Routinely inspecting your book's business execution and advertising viability can give experiences into what methodologies are working and what might require change.

1. Deals Information Examination

•Dissect your business information to distinguish patterns, top deals periods, and likely regions for development.

2. Showcasing Adequacy

•Audit the presentation of your promoting efforts to comprehend which channels and messages have been best in driving deals.

Supporting book deals after the underlying send off requires progressing exertion, innovativeness, and variation to changing business sector elements. By drawing in with your crowd consistently, executing standard limited time crusades, utilizing surveys, investigating extra income streams, keeping your substance new, and routinely dissecting your exhibition, you can keep up with energy and make long haul progress for your book.

# 12

# Chapter 12: Planning Your Next Steps

After effectively distributing and supporting deals for your book, it's vital to begin looking forward and arranging your following stages. This part offers direction on the most proficient method to use your ongoing accomplishment into future undertakings, whether it be continuations, a series, or completely new pursuits. Arranging your subsequent stages with vital foreknowledge can assist with guaranteeing proceeded with progress and development in your composing vocation.

Assessing Your Ongoing Achievement

Prior to jumping into new ventures, carve out opportunity to assess the progress of your ongoing book. Understanding what functioned admirably and what could be further developed will give important experiences to future undertakings.

1. Survey Criticism and Deals Information

•Examine peruser criticism and deals information to distinguish the qualities and shortcomings of your book. This can direct the course of your next project.

2. Market and Crowd Examination

•Survey the market and your ideal interest group's ongoing advantages. Consider how patterns could have moved since your last distribution and what these progressions could mean for your next project.

Laying out Objectives for Your Next Venture

Clear, reachable objectives can give guidance and inspiration for your next project. Consider what you expect to accomplish, both inventively and industrially.

1. Innovative Desires

•Think about your own innovative objectives. Whether it's investigating new classifications, subjects, or composing styles, figure out what you need to accomplish with your next project.

2. Business Goals

•Set explicit business goals, for example, deals targets, crowd development, or getting a distributing bargain. These will shape your advertising and circulation techniques.

Fostering Your Next Undertaking

With a reasonable comprehension of your past progress and future objectives, start arranging your next project. This could include developing your ongoing work or investigating novel thoughts.

1. Continuations and Series

•On the off chance that your book has the potential for spin-offs or a series, consider how to extend its universe. Plan the all-encompassing account and how every portion will add to it.

2. New Undertakings

•For altogether new activities, begin with conceptualizing and research. Search for holes on the lookout or interesting points you can investigate.

Expanding on Your Prosperity

Utilize the force from your ongoing accomplishment to support your next project. Influence your laid out crowd, stage, and industry associations.

1. Connect with Your Current Crowd

•Keep your ongoing perusers connected through online entertainment, email pamphlets, and individual appearances. Begin building expectation for your next project right off the bat.

2. Use Your Foundation

•Utilize your creator stage to share updates, secrets, and in the background checks your forthcoming venture out. This can assist with keeping up with interest and commitment.

3. Network and Team up

•Keep on systems administration with industry experts and investigate joint effort open doors. These associations can offer important help and openness for your next project.

Anticipating Distribution and Then some

As you foster your next project, begin anticipating its distribution and the way that you will support its prosperity post-send off.

1. Distribution Procedure

•Settle on your distribution course (conventional, independently publishing, half breed) early and plan likewise. Think about timetables, advertising procedures, and any likely difficulties.

2. Showcasing and Advancement

•Foster a showcasing and advancement plan customized to your venture. Consider what methodologies functioned admirably previously and how they can be adjusted or extended.

3. Long haul Profession Arranging

•Consider how your next project squeezes into your drawn out profession objectives. Plan for ceaseless learning, expertise improvement, and ways of extending your scope as a creator.

Arranging your subsequent stages after an effective book send off is pivotal for keeping up with energy and building a manageable composing vocation. By assessing your ongoing achievement, laying out clear objectives, fostering your next project with vital preparation, and utilizing your laid out stage, you can keep on developing as a creator and make more prominent progress with each new undertaking.

9 798869 334859